First published 2020 by Modern Toss Ltd.
www.moderntoss.com

ISBN: 978-0-9929107-9-2

Text and illustrations copyright © Modern Toss Limited, 2020
Modern Toss, 415 Linen Hall, 162-168 Regent Street, London W1B 5TE

A CIP catalogue record for this book is available from the British Library.

Designed and typeset by Modern Toss

Visit www.moderntoss.com to read more about all our books and to buy them yeah.
You will also find lots of other shit there, and you can sign up to our mailing list so
that you're always kept bang up to date with it, cheers.

Modern Toss *presents*

COLLECTED WORKS

from

Drive-By Abuser

2020

foreword

Drive-by Abuser considers a collection of his own work

Alright?
what are you ?
a buffet of thought nibbles
reverse honked straight into your guts
then sprayed out of both ends
onto the pages of a book
must all be classics yeah?
I should know
I fucking wrote them.

Sunbather

Laying out in the sun yeah
it's alright for some innit
I expect you'll get up in bit
rub on a bit of cream
re-arrange your towel
see if anyone's looking at you
then lie down for another hour
let's hope we're not relying
on cunts like you
to kickstart the economy.

———

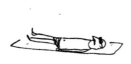

The Farmer

Alright! You a farmer yeah?
foot and mouth an' all that?
what you sellin'?
big lumps of torn-off meat?
expect you're up at half past three, aren'tcha?
watching all the animals
honking and shitting themselves...
good luck to ya
I couldn't fucking do it...

Ready Meal

Edible shit box
with a plastic sheet on top?
got to peel it off yeah,
or pop it with a fork
you lazy fucker
survival of the fittest?
not in your case mate.

TV Quipster

Quipping about things
riffing with your wit
sipping your water
everytime you get a laugh
you fucking cunt.

Texting

Sending a text?
leving out som leters yeah
doing it relly fckin fast yeah
why not eh
dnt cost fuck al does it
asking someone if their alrght?
trns out yeah, they R
at least u fucking know
give yourself a break
or ull end up with thumb cancer
have to use ur tongue then
get all spit in the buttons:).

The Gardener

Telling all the plants where to grow?
pulling out the ones you don't like the look of
then burning 'em on a fire
not far off Pol Pot are you?
when you think about it.

The Swan

You king of the ducks mate?
yeah looks like it an' all
reckon yourself a bit don't you
giving it all that with your big fucking neck
tell you what, if I ever drop me keys down the drain
you can come and fish 'em out for me
you got a business card? or shall I just look you up
under "stuck up pond toff"
see ya round yeah.

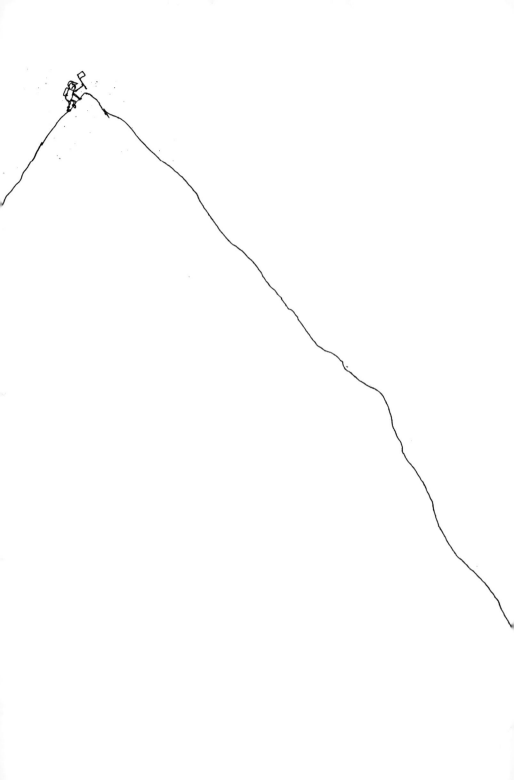

The Mountaineer

Pushing yourself to the limits of human endurance
climbing up a big dirt pile
take a picture when you get to the top
so we all know you're not bullshitting it yeah
then come back down
and wank on about it
for the rest of your life
ever tried working in an office?
doubt you're up to it mate
but someone's got to do it.

The Cloud

Sucking all the moisture up from one place
then randomly floating off somewhere else
and pissing it out all over the shop
without a care in the world?
you're living the dream mate.

The Furrier

What you using ocelot?
got to hose the guts out first
it's only little innit
probably get an arm out of it
fiddly fucking job yeah
still, get its arsehole in the right place
and you'll be able to put a button through it
makes sense don't it.

Ornithologist

Hiding in bushes yeah
spying on birds
ticking 'em off in a little book?
still there's no law against it is there?
be different if it was people though wouldn't it.
you'd be banged up
with all the fucking perverts.

The Tree

You a tree yeah ?!
big pole made out of wood
crawling with fucking insects
alright for some innit!
shedding your shit everywhere
hope you're gonna clear all that up
do you want a dustpan and brush?
nah, didn't think so..
what's your 'Autumn Look' gonna be?
same as last year? bunch of fucking twigs?
yeah, you carry on mate
see ya round yeah!

The Internet

Alright,
you a big digital shit cloud
of wrong information
and photos of people fucking each other?
that'd be a trip up to the library
in the old days
cheers.

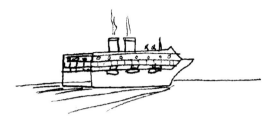

Cruise Ship

Alright, you a big floating piss machine yeah?
packed out with old people
on a last minute death trip
I expect most of em'll be
coming back in the freezer
won't they?
ah chuck 'em overboard mate
no one's looking.

Shopping

Doing some shopping are ya?
carrying it home yeah
in some little bags?
getting it out, yeah?
sticking it on a fucking shelf ?
pay for it later love,
it's all a load of bollocks innit
whack it on the plastic!

The Chair

Square wooden platform,
supported by four sticks
with an upright plank acting as a back rest
sometimes with arm supports
sometimes without yeah
often covered in a patterned cloth of some sort
or completely moulded out of plastic
whatever the fuck you're made out of
you're always there helping maintain a position
halfway between standing up and lying down
try doing that without a chair
probably end up shitting yourself after six seconds
see you round yeah.

The Artist

Doing a painting of it are ya?
capturing the moment on canvas yeah?
what is it acrylics?
gotta sketch it out first haven't ya
then put the colours on and that
you wanna get a fucking life don't ya?
bet it looks like a stack of old shit
see ya!

Meeting

Sat in a room yeah
with some people
banging some ideas around
took four weeks to get everyone together
better think of something to say
or people will think you're fucking thick.

Golf

Mate! Oi mate!
what you playing golf are ya? yeah?
yeah, fucking looks like it an' all
where you get the jumper from?
no, not saying?
well good luck to ya, cos I wouldn't have
the fucking nerve
tell you what, leave it eh
I'll let you get on.

Country House

Alright mate! country house are ya?
looks like it an'all
giving it all that with your windows and columns
like some big fucking chinless shed
nice spot you got yourself, innit
who's ya owner, Baron Lord Dave Fontleroy?
nah, made it up mate
stick with it, yeah
Rule Bri-fucking-tania!
see ya 'round!

Wearing a hat

Wearing a hat yeah?
keeps the sun off
and tells people
that you're an arsehole
kill two birds with one stone
everyone's a winner.

Posting a Letter

Posting a letter yeah?
sticking a bit of paper in a hole
hoping some idiot
can be bothered to deliver it?
second class?
might as well tear it up
and fucking eat it
least you get a meal out of it
I'm off to check me emails
see ya round grandad!

Sunday Walk

Going for a Sunday walk?
gets you out of the house don't it
stretch your fucking legs
what's on the telly?
nothing
mind that bit of shit.

The Hotel

Alright hotel yeah?
big building full of people
watching porn and fucking each other
electric kettle and a plate
of biscuits in every room?
it's alright for some innit

had any famous people in?
why don't you scrape up some of
their carpet hair and sell it
could be anyone's though couldn't it
maybe get 'em to sign it or do so some
sort of forensic test shit on it
they might want paying then,

I don't fucking know
you work out the small print yeah,
see ya.

People Saying Sorry

Alright, you just said sorry to someone
'cos they bumped into you?
you need to recalibrate your
response to shit like that yeah?
what are you gonna do if they punch you in the face?
offer to cook their fucking dinner or something?
sorry mate, I'm only joking
it's a fucking minefield yeah?
see you 'round.

sorry

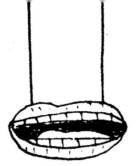

The Mouth

You a mouth yeah?
stuck on the front of a face
normally down at the bottom innit
words coming out
food going in
keep it that way round
or you'll get in a right fucking mess.

Telephone Box

Alright! What you doing in there?
having a piss or ringing up a prostitute?
got to be one or the other, hasn't it?
why not though, eh, it's your life, innit
ah, good luck to ya mate
see ya 'round yeah.

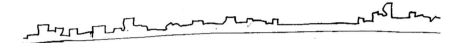

The Seagull

Alright mate, seagull yeah?
mastering the art of flying
whilst shitting yourself
I bet it's not as easy as it looks,
a bit like playing the violin
I couldn't do it, and not for want of trying
still don't let people belittle it mate
most of them couldn't even walk and shit themselves
they're just fucking jealous, stick with it yeah.

The Newspaper Reader

Reading a newspaper?
catching up on the latest developments
of all the shit that's going on?
I expect the world rests easier
knowing you're up to speed with it all
I get it all online mate
not that I can be bothered most of the time
unless some footballer's fucked
a prostitute or something
turns out they have, I'm off to
check the latest see you around yeah!

Football

Alright, football?
kicking the ball in the net
then having a little cheer and a kiss about it?
not exactly fucking chess, is it!
why not though, eh!
it's your life innit. I'll let you get on with it
'offside!' yeah!
just kidding, I haven't got a clue mate
see ya round yeah.

The Flag

Bit of cloth yeah?
flapping about on top of a pole all day
don't know how you do it mate
must be bored out of your fucking tits
mind you if someone dies
they let you down a bit,
something to look forward to innit.

Walking a dog

You walking a dog yeah?
got to let it out 'int ya
fucking sniffs a lot don't it
every two fucking steps
oh it's having a piss now
remember your shit bags?
don't want to pay a 500 quid fine
for a bit of shit that you
didn't even technically do
catch you later yeah.

Brie

Big old fucking lump
of triangular fat
don't leave it out in the sun
fucking melts like a piece of shit
you have to chuck it away
that's what happened to me anyway, cheers.

The Fast Moving News Event

Alright?
something big happened has it?
better get online, make some comment about it
quick elbow your way in,
it's like the fucking Harrods sale yeah
this could be your breakthrough comment
know anyone you can test it out on?
probably not yeah?
just bang it up in case it's good

fucksake hang on!
looks like you've spelt a basic word wrong
you're the laughing stock of the forum
good job you haven't got the bottle
to use your real name
you fucking sad cunt.

The Archaelogical Dig

Alright, digging up some everyday shit
from 1000s of years ago?
what you found, a pot that people used to piss in?
what else you got, an ancient flip flop made of goat skin
you gonna charge people to look at it in a museum?
d'you reckon anyone's going to be
digging up your shit in a 1000 years?
probably recycled it all yeah?
Not so fucking clever now are you.

Alfresco Diner

Sitting at a little table on the pavement
eating a plate of food are you?
trying to look like you do it all time
it's the new thing though innit
bit of continental flavour yeah
any idiot can sit indoors can't they?
have to bang it down quick though
in case a bird shits on it.

The Urban Fox

Alright mate, licking out a dustbin yeah?
honked up leftovers on a bed of disposable nappies?
that'd cost a fucking packet at a cutting edge eatery
still at least it's cooked,
out in the country you'd be spending half your time
trapping your own food and picking the shit
out of its guts.

Well done for embracing
the 24/7 convenience lifestyle,
maybe if all endangered animals
took a leaf out of your book
they wouldn't all be living on fucking handouts.

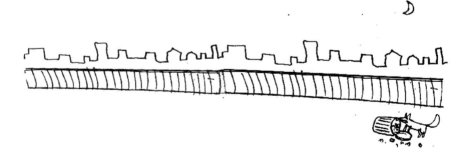

Gastropub

Alright?
what the fuck are you then?
a restaurant or a pub?
still, get 'em pissed up enough
then they can't blame the food
while they're spraying their guts out
all over your car park.

Power Station

Alright! you generating power to keep
everyone's gadgets and nik-naks going?
yeah, looks like it an' all
don't get me wrong, I've got the lot
computer, toaster, electric toothbrush
you name it, I've fucking got it
I tell you what mate, if it wasn't for you we'd all
be back in the stone age eating our own shit
not that I've got anything against that
nah, you're doing a good job mate
stick with it yeah
I'll let you get on.

The Jogger

What you running from?
a made up image of yourself
as the world's fattest man
tucking into a grab bag of cheese and onion
cathetered up to a bucket
and then winched out by a crane when you die...
Probably get a TV programme out of that.

Sainsbury's Homebase

New branch of homebase?
that's handy
where's your shower nozzles mate?
I expect they're over the back somewhere yeah
I might come back later
do a doughnut in the car park.

The Christmas Tree

Seasonal tree are you?
pointless existence innit
sitting round like a cunt all year
then some bloke digs you up
and puts you in a bucket
couple of weeks later
you're slung out
in a bag full of turkey fat
not much of a way
to start the new year is it?

Picnic

Having a little picnic are ya?
ham, cheese, packet of crisps.
cooler bag for it yeah?
nice day for it
why not eh?
you make me fucking sick
see ya.

The Print

Alright?
Looking at a limited edition print yeah?
Peering at it, close up.
It's got some words on it,
looks like it might contain
some sort of poignant statement
about life or something.
Oh no, it's just bollocks
how much d'you pay for it
about 70 quid? Not bad yeah,
might be worth a couple of mil one day,
fucking doubt it though
cheers yeah.

Reindeer

Alright! pack of reindeer yeah?
dragging a big old sack
of Christmas nik-naks
while some bloke whips
your arsehole with a stick?
still it's only once a year innit...

Traffic Light

You a traffic light yeah?
yeah fucking looks like it an' all
changing colours
red, amber, green
limited range, innit
making a little beeping noise
for all the blind people
nice of ya...
beep beep beep beep... green man!
oh, he's red now!
you're stuck in a rut
see ya round, yeah.

New Year Disco

Alright?
waiting for Big Ben
to tell you you've just shitted another year
of your life up the fucking wall?
Still at least your're not sat indoors
texting your cousin an emoji.

The Cappucino

Think you're fucking it don't you?
little cup, half-full of hot brown shit
topped off with a lump
of frothed up cow's piss
sling on a bit of brown dust
don't sound so appealing does it?
when you put it like that
probably why you got a fancy fucking name
you stuck up cunt.

The Matchstick

Little strip of wood yeah
one end of you caked in phosphorus shit
sitting still as fuck in a box
twenty four seven,
three six five
waiting for the day
to get your tip scraped
against the box you live in
till your head explodes
that's life mate,
don't come running to me.

see ya 'round yeah